I0002814

Jack Covert, Founder and President 800-CEO-READ

"Your relationship with your customer doesn't have to be over the minute they leave your establishment or website. Social media services such as Twitter allow you to continue your good service beyond the point of sale, create long-lasting relationships, and reap the kind of unparalleled customer loyalty that only good two-way communication can build. Not sure where to start? I read a lot of business books and I can tell you TwitterWorks has all the answers provided by guys who have walked the walk."

Chris Brogan, New York Times Bestselling Author
Social Media 101 and Trust Agents

"Phil, Joe, and Scott are the right guys to write this book because they LIVE THIS STUFF. There, that's 140 characters. Well, actually it's a lot less than 140, because you need room to let people retweet. And you really need room to let people comment. And to be honest, if YOU are checking this book out, I'm going to say you didn't really know you needed that. And that's the point. Read TwitterWorks and save yourself 8 months of apologizing for learning on the job."

Mark Brandau, Senior Desk Editor - Nation's Restaurant News

"Smart restaurateurs like the authors of 'TwitterWorks' know that the value of social media lies in the "social", rather than the "media." Whether the platform is Twitter, Foursquare or whatever comes next, social media presents one of the easiest, most cost-effective ways to speak to your customers and, more importantly, listen to them. Operators can learn a lot from the stories of their tenacious peers in this book."

Becky McCray, publisher of www.smallbizsurvival.com

"From the first moment you read the disclaimer, you know this is going to be a useful book. The stories lead you to tips you'll use over and over in your business. Nothing else levels the playing field for the restaurant and small business industry like social media. And no one explains these new marketing methods like Phil, Joe and Scott, because they come right in with the perspective of people in the business PLUS the customer's perspective."

Why should I buy this book?

Very simply, Twitter works.

Compared to traditional advertising, Twitter is just as effective, much less expensive (in fact, it's basically free) and a better investment because it has a much faster return on investment.

As restaurant owners ourselves, we have seen first-hand how it can increase business. And the funny thing is, we just happened upon Twitter. But once we did, we found tremendous success in utilizing it to communicate with our patrons, increase brand awareness and grow our business.

Most importantly, we believe Twitter can help your restaurant business.

How? Read on.

Level the playing field. Leverage your control as an independent operator to compete with the large corporate chains that have large corporate adverting budgets – they simply cannot engage their guests in this way, nor can they react with the speed their guests need – these tools will allow you to do.

Beat the recession. One of the greatest attributes of the tools in this book is that they are free. There is no cost to utilize them other than your own time, and you can find some of that to improve your business, no?

Improve your restaurant. The one common denominator of every restaurant is that it exists entirely for the guests' enjoyment. The tools in this book will allow you to solicit their feedback in a fun and non-intrusive way. But it will be up to you to use that feedback to improve your guests' experience.

Rebuild your restaurant. Okay, so you've made some mistakes in your business. Everyone does. The tools in this book will facilitate transparency. They will allow you to get out in front of your mistakes and ask your guests for their forgiveness and their business – all in one simple style of communication.

WARNING
DO NOT
use the tactics
in this book!

If you do not have something
you completely believe in.

DANGER

MAKE SURE YOUR
systems are already
in place: costs, labor,
business processes.

⚠ CAUTION

Tactics in this book
will shine a spotlight
on your products,
service and business.

Social Media Has Changed Everything.

by Steffan Antonas

"The Internet is changing our relationship with technology and the way we market our businesses. Social networks now have more influence over consumer buying decisions than any other marketing tool. Smart businesses are adopting new online tools and strategies to adapt with their customers, and those that aren't are falling behind. Because the nature of their business is inherently social, restaurants in particular have an unparalleled opportunity to tap into the power of social networks to grow their bottom line. But be warned, it's not just about new technology. Winning in this new digital age demands that restaurant owners embrace a completely new approach to dealing with customers and doing business. This new approach is more transparent, interactive and is above all, very human.

TwitterWorks is an indispensable handbook for anyone wanting to understand this new approach. It explains what it will take for restaurants to thrive in this challenging new environment. You won't get any smoke and mirrors in these pages. Just practical advice and tactics that work. Not only will you learn how to use a new arsenal of free tools

to connect with your customers, you'll learn how to leverage these tools to find out what your customers are saying about you, how to find and entice new customers to your tables, and how to build exciting experiences for them that accelerates word of mouth. Whether you're a new restaurant owner or a seasoned veteran of the industry, this book will give you all the tools and strategies you need to feel like you can get out there and embrace social media and execute your own marketing strategies in an honest, effective and profitable way.

I can't think of three more qualified guys than Joe, Phil and Scott to teach you the new rules of how to run a restaurant. They are pioneers who've taken what they've learned from their efforts to integrate these new tools into their own businesses and combined it with their understanding of what it takes to run a successful restaurant to help you better understand the mindset and strategies you need to succeed. Listen carefully to them and learn from their stories. They aren't self-appointed gurus trying to make a buck. They've actually lived it."

- **Steffan Antonas, steffanantonas.com**

Notes:

#TwitterWorks – Level the playing field. Beat the recession. Improve your restaurant. Rebuild your restaurant. Whatever you want to do with Twitter, you can, but you need to have a strategy and you need to know the tools. This book will help you do all of this, and more!

#TwitterWorks

Foreward by: Steffan Antonas. Illustrations by: Mike Rohde and Scott Baitinger. Photography by: Olga Thomas, Scott Baitinger, Joe Sorge and others. Edited by: Julie Tramonte, Angie Sorge, Janet Fox Driscoll and over 50 of our twitter followers.

2nd Edition

ISBN: 1452818681
EAN-13: 9781452818689

Published 1/2011 by:
2.0 Books, A Publishing Company

Your customers interact through social media. Does your restaurant?

This fabulous illustration, by Mike Rohde (@rohdesign), depicts the transition from traditional communication (Restaurant 1.0) to a two-way style of communication (Restaurant 2.0) using Twitter and social media.

Essentially, Restaurant 1.0 is how we've all learned to operate and advertise our businesses. We promote our opening to the world, place "help wanted" advertisements, build a website to showcase our hours and menus and perhaps provide links to glorious reviews and a phone number for reservations. Basically, it provides all the one-way communication our potential guests might need to actually make it to our restaurant and enjoy a meal with us.

Enter Restaurant 2.0. She is a much different animal. And while she begins her life looking exactly the same as Restaurant 1.0 (as you can see in the illustration), it's how she travels along a timeline that changes and shapes the business itself. Here's a twist to the theory of "build it and they will come." Under this new business model, we have an opportunity to custom build a restaurant exactly the way our guests want it. The earlier this process begins, the more beneficial it can be for your restaurant.

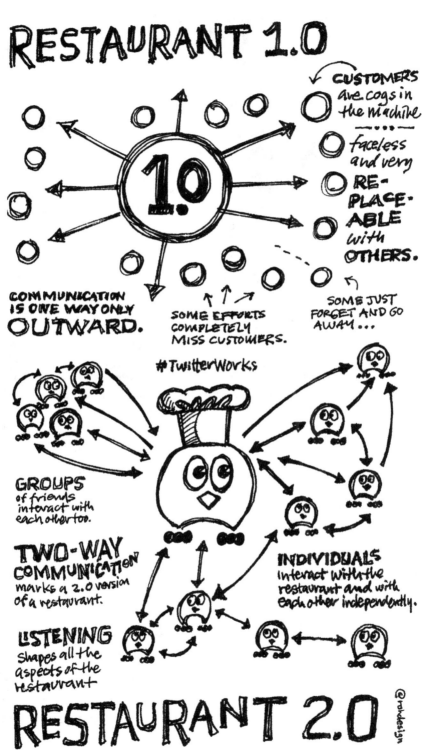

Two-way communication is what makes Restaurant 2.0 work. Not only communication between the restaurant and customers, but between customers and their friends.

See how the business in the illustration is shaped and transformed by its interaction with its guests. This process can begin even before your business completes its first transaction. In the case of Streetza Pizza, potential customers even helped pick a logo before they opened for business! (More on Streetza Pizza later.)

This strategy has been proven to work as your business continues operating on a daily basis. For instance, our guests at AJ Bombers in Milwaukee have provided feedback and played an integral role in shaping our décor, our pricing structure, promotions, menu items and the kind of beverages we carry. They have even helped us to decide how late we should keep our doors open on any given night of the week! The more they've become involved, the more interested they are in our restaurant's success because it's effectively their restaurant. And – surprise, surprise – the more successful AJ Bombers has become.

I cannot overstate the fact that we did NOT set out to employ these methods as a tactic to grow our business. This is the story of what happened to a couple of restaurant owners who chose to listen to their customers and actually give them what they were asking for. It wasn't until our businesses began to grow unusually fast, in perhaps the worst economic conditions our generation has known, that we started to notice it was our guests who were actually in control. And we loved it even more than they did. Our gratitude for the personal and professional lessons they have taught us is difficult to put in to words.

We hope that you can adapt many of the tips and stories in this book to help grow your business. You have the guests already, I'm guessing. Hopefully, this book will show you how to engage them a bit more openly by using Twitter and other social media tools.

With the advancements in technology, word-of-mouth is instantanious, and includes video and photos. It's now more powerful than ever.

Notes:

#TwitterWorks – Find new customers, fans and friends by building awareness.

#TwitterWorks

#TwitterWorks - Chapter 2

What is Twitter?

This section will give you the basic information you need to learn the power of our platform of choice.

According to Twitter: Twitter is a real-time information network, powered by people all around the world, that lets you share and discover what's happening now.

Twitter asks, "What's happening?" and spreads the answer across the globe to millions, immediately.

If you ask me:

That's all Twitter is, in 140 characters or less. But that probably doesn't help you, if you have no idea what Twitter is. If you do, that's all you need to know. If not, let me break that down for you:

"Twitter is a micro-blogging platform."

By this, I mean Twitter is a smaller scale place to share your thoughts, ideas, and insights as compared to a full-on blog, article, newsletter, magazine, TV/radio show or commercial. You need a headline or a hook that grabs people, that makes them interested in learning more about you, your product, what you're selling, the questions you have, and the solution you're offering. It's rarely over-edited, though some take their time to craft something really catchy. It's up to you how to do that, but remember to focus on what's in it for your audience. Focus on the benefits, not the features. But be brief about it.

Twitter is a place to share and find anything.

You can share photos, graphics, links, videos, thoughts, ideas, people, and links – whatever you want people to find.

The key to Twitter is the context in which something is shared. If someone you don't trust sends you an envelope in the mail that says, "You may have already won $100 million. Open immediately for details!" and no more information can be found on the outside of the envelope, do you rush to open it? Or, do you throw it out, realizing it's probably just junk mail? The same is true with Twitter.

At first, you have no context. You don't know anyone so you don't trust anything anyone says. I had this experience for almost 6 months. I followed few people, never clicked on any links for fear of getting a virus, and kept to myself. So Twitter was a waste of my time. Then one day I was at a conference, and everyone there was using Twitter. I started following these people I'd met in real life, and the people they recommended, and other people they recommended, and suddenly I realized the power of Twitter.

Find someone you trust to get information from and listen to them. Copy how they do things, though not exactly what they do, and work to find your own voice.

This clicked in for me when there were only about 1 million people using Twitter. There are now over 75 million people using Twitter. With more signing up every second.

There are many more basics of Twitter. If you want to learn a lot more, we recommend you check out: http://business.twitter.com/twitter101/

Or Mashable's Twitter guidebook at http://mashable.com/guidebook/twitter

Once you start twittering, make sure to let everyone know about it. Put your @ symbol on everything you can, menus, packaging and even your building.

Notes:

#TwitterWorks – With 12 million users, if you work hard and say something interesting, you can get traditional media coverage and reach an entirely different audience.

#TwitterWorks

What is Twitter to a restaurant?

(What did you have for dinner, and why should I care?)

To better answer that question, here's an example of how a tweet can go from boring to marketing:

scottbait

I had a sandwich at my house. Alone. My life sucks.

less than 20 seconds ago via web

Nobody cares about what you had for dinner…unless you include some context about it. Did you eat at a new local place with some amazing people, customers, potential customers or partners, and have a great conversation that you'd like to tease people with? If so, you can turn this into a SUPER interesting tweet.

Let's add some context:

See how I've gone from the mundane, i.e., talking about what I had for dinner, to something more relevant? The tweet becomes much more interesting because now I'm talking about something other folks may want to learn more about, or at least peak some interest. Additionally, if the other two people, or the location I mentioned are active on Twitter, they may share it with their Twitter network, exposing me to more Twitter people and letting people in their network know that we have a relationship.

Twitter lets you be you – when you aren't there.

Because you're likely already in the restaurant or hospitality business, we're going to go ahead and assume that you like people in general, enjoy the premise of service in general, and would genuinely like nothing more than to please your guests. **Great news!** Twitter is simply an extension of the service style of your restaurant. Speak to your guests on Twitter just as you would if they were visiting you in your own business. Say hello, welcome them and ask about how their visit with you was today. Thank them for their business! You will be amazed at how far a simple acknowledgement can go. After all, this is a business of service and warm interactions in the end, and that's all your guests really want from you (and great food, of course.) You CAN offer that same personal service on Twitter with very little effort.

Still not sold completely?

Here are some stats on Twitter.

Maybe these statistics will convince you of the OCEAN of users (make that potential patrons!) you could be interacting and engaging with. And the good news is that you're not too late. Twitter is still in its infancy with many users still not fully understanding how to utilize its power. (See, you're not alone!)

In December 2009, Twitter had over 75 million user accounts.

The monthly rate of new user accounts peaked in July 2009, and now there are around 6.2 million new accounts per month (or 2-3 per second). This is about 20% below July 2009's peak rate.

A large percentage of Twitter accounts are inactive, with about 25% of accounts having no followers, and about 40% of accounts having never sent a single Tweet.

Only about 17% of registered Twitter accounts sent a tweet in December 2009, an all-time low.

Despite these facts, Twitter users are becoming more engaged over time when we control for sample age. In fact, a study from PRWeek and PR Newswire found that about 70 percent of PR pitches conducted through social media result in coverage.

We share these stats with you to encourage you, and show you that the bar is incredibly low to making Twitter work for your restaurant. And yes, you CAN make Twitter work for your restaurant. Trust us!

Source: http://themetricsystem.rjmetrics.com/2010/01/26/new-data-on-twitters-users-and-engagement/
http://multivu.prnewswire.com/mnr/prnewswire/43321/

Twitter Dictionary:

Before we get ahead of ourselves, let's define some Twitter terms so we're all on the same page. If your business is already a heavy Twitter user you may want to skip this section. (But don't worry, you haven't wasted your money buying this book.)

Cotag – Signature of one user in a multi-user-account like ^BS at the end of a tweet to signify who created the tweet. Important note: Put the full names of the people in your bio so folks know who BS is.

Direct Message (DM) – A private tweet to someone who follows you. If you don't follow them back, they can't reply to you.

Follower – Someone who has subscribed to your tweets. You may send a direct message (DM) which is a private message to anyone who is a follower of yours using the Twitter messaging system.

FollowFriday – (#FollowFriday) was started by Micah Baldwin (@micah) in January 2009 as a way for Twitter users to recommend people who they enjoy following to their own followers. As is typical of social media, FollowFriday immediately went "viral" and became a global phenomenon. Put the #FollowFriday (or #FF) hash in your message to let others know you're sharing knowledgeable people that they should follow.

FollowLocals – A tag used on Twitter as a way to tell your LOCAL followers about other LOCAL Twitterers who are worth following. Put the #FollowLocals hash-tag in your message to let others know you're sharing knowledgeable LOCAL people they should follow.

Following – Following someone means you will see their tweets (Twitter updates) in your personal timeline. Twitter lets you see who you follow, and who is following you. Followers are people who receive other people's Twitter updates.

Timeline – Twitter timeline is a twitter visualization tool that allows you to view your twitter feed in a timeline format.

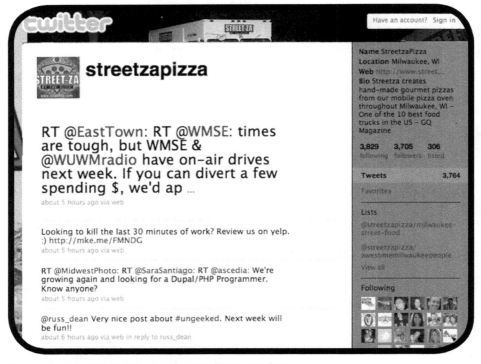

Pictured above: The Twitter timeline for @StreetzaPizza.

Twansformer – An application that modifies your tweet before you send it. Examples: spell check, shortening URLs or conversion to text-speak so it fits under 140 characters are twansformers.

Twanslator – An application that enables you to translate your tweets or other people's tweets into another language.

Tweet – This is the formal name for messages sent through Twitter, or the act of posting to Twitter. Tweets are in the public Twitter timeline, and anyone can see and search for what you shared unless you protect your updates.

Tweetback – A backlink tweet for a blog article.

Tweeter – A Twitter user; a person who tweets.

Protect your updates – Protecting your updates is something people do when they want to share their tweets only with people they've allowed in. This is like talking in a closet, and we would NEVER recommend anyone do this. If you want to protect your tweets, don't use Twitter.

@PeterWilt1 hmm, it's possible yes. Let's ask @msorge
29 minutes ago via HootSuite in reply to PeterWilt1

@ – When used at the beginning of a tweet, when coupled with a username, it's directing a message AT someone (@ sign)

@ – When used inside a Tweet, and coupled with a username, means the message is ABOUT someone (@ sign references a person.)

RT – Re-Tweet – to take what someone else tweeted and repost it to share it with your followers.

 # (hashtag) – A way of signifying a topic or channel of conversation. Can be clicked to immediately take you to the Twitter search for every tweet using that hashtag.

URL shortener – A service that allows you to take a long URL and make it smaller. Some offer statistics (like http://bit.ly) and some do not (like http://is.gd).

MKE.me

Milwaukee's Own Link-Shortener

http://

(Make A Shorter URL!)

Powered by MilwaukeeFood.com ©2010

MKE.me, a popular Milwaukee link shortener.

Notes:

#TwitterWorks – Even when you're not there, or you don't have time, to make a relationship work face to face.

#TwitterWorks

Twitter 101.

The goal of this section is to give you enough basic information to help you start using Twitter. These are not advanced topics, but rather things you can do to begin using Twitter for your business.

Sign Up: Obviously, you have to sign up for Twitter to use it, though if you want to just listen, you can go to http://search.twitter.com and "listen" for anything your heart desires. Listening on a social media service, like Twitter, involves monitoring your restaurant's name, your special menu items, your name and any of your influential employees. While you can "listen" to anything you want, if you narrow the listening down to 5 or 6 terms, you'll be more effective than if you try to listen to every possible way customers and potential customers talk about your business.

Most of the power of Twitter is in signing up however. When you sign up, you'll get to add some characteristics that make the site uniquely yours.

Username: It's best to pick a username that is as close to your own name as possible. Include a middle initial if necessary, or go long (or short). Picking the restaurant name is also great, especially if you own a few restaurants. Add the word "rest" in your username at the end if your name is already taken, or include an _ (underscore) if you have to. The more memorable the name, the better. Remember: Spelling counts!

Name: Use the full name of your restaurant. You get up to 20 characters. Abbreviate where obvious, but spell out most if possible.

Location: Joe includes a link to his Google map. Scott has Milwaukee, WI. Others have a combination of a city, state, and a part of town, like East Side Milwaukee or Downtown Indianapolis. You do what feels best for you.

Bio: 160 characters are all you get. Think about what information people may want to know in a restaurant search. This is your chance to tell people about your restaurant, locations, offerings – all in 160 characters. Include your specialty dishes. Add a cool saying if you want to. Think of it as a mini ad.

Take the Streetza Pizza bio, for example: "Streetza creates handmade gourmet pizzas from our mobile pizza oven throughout Milwaukee, WI - One of the 10 best food trucks in the US - GQ Magazine"

Here's AJ Bombers' bio: "Voted Milwaukee's best new burger joint, smoke free and loads of p-nut bombs. Where everybody knows your name. Well, at least your Twitter name."

Photo: If you include a photo, it will automatically be resized down to 73 x 73 by Twitter – but don't use a small picture yourself. Use a square picture, up to the maximum size of 700k. Note that it can be a .jpg, .gif or .png, which is nice because then you can include your logo or your personal photo. Joe and Scott both use pictures of their logos. Phil has a personal photo. Use whichever makes the most sense for you. If you use a photo, make sure it's a good one.

Link: Include a link to your restaurant's website (you DO have a restaurant website, don't you?? If not, we won't judge you, or tell you how to fix that in THIS book. Maybe some other time.), or somewhere folks can find out more about you online. Some people even create a special "Twitter followers" page where folks can click and get special deals. That's cool, too!

Background image: In our opinion, this is the underutilized piece of real estate on Twitter! Though nothing on the background is clickable, this is a great opportunity to list your hours of operation, a map, high quality pictures of your restaurant, or photos of your staff and/or customers. You can do a left-hand column-only background (make it about 200 pixels large), or a full-page background (1600 x 1200 pixels is about right). Try a few times to make this right for you. There are a LOT of places to create a free background.

Three of our favorites are
• http://www.twitrbackgrounds.com/
• http://twilk.com/
• http://www.twitbacks.com/

If you'd rather have a consistent look and feel with your restaurant's website, have a graphic designer do one to match your restaurant's main theme.

Diagramming a tweet and Twitter vocabulary

**RT @Scobleizer: Ouch, I guess this Austin bar owner doesn't like blog-
gers: http://bit.ly/cJe32R thanks @ekai // Wow! Someone doesn't get it!**

Let's take an in-depth look at the six compenents of this tweet.

1. RT (ReTweet) – this tweet was originally from someone else

2. @Scobleizer – the originator of the tweet

3. Ouch, I guess this Austin bar owner doesn't like bloggers: - this is the
headline/teaser for a photo/link/video.

4. http://bit.ly/cJe32R - the URL to something too large to share via
Twitter (Could be a picture, video, or anything else.)

5. http://bit.ly - this indicates a URL shortener was used. The actual
URL linked to is http://www.flickr.com/photos/ekai/4448924106/sizes/o/
(which is too long for Twitter if you want to say something about it).

6. @ – Thanking @ekai for the link within the tweet.

#TwitterWorks – With 12 million users, if you work hard and say something interesting, you can get traditional media coverage and reach an entirely different audience.

#TwitterWorks

The 30-minute Twitter solution.

Once you start using Twitter and get comfortable with it, if you're not careful, you could be on Twitter literally ALL DAY LONG. And if that happens, you won't get any real work done, so you'll drive your business directly into the ground.

Thankfully, there's a better option. We call it the 30-Minute Twitter Solution, and you can use it to connect with your customers and potential customers in just 30 minutes a day (hence the name) to drive your business forward.

In order for the 30-Minute Twitter Solution to work, you will be required to set it up, which may take you 30 minutes in itself.

There's only one tool required to make this work, and that's HootSuite. Go to http://hootsuite.com and set up a free account. It's the best free tool out there and it will be perfect for your 30-minute Twitter needs. (Once you set it up, all you need to do is log onto HootSuite on any computer (PC or Macintosh) and all of your work will be saved.)

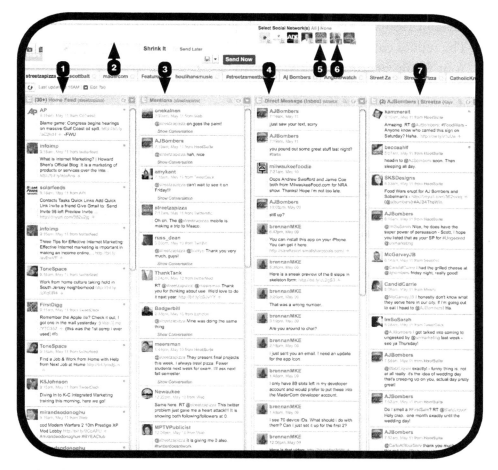

Let's take an quick look at the seven components of HootSuite.

1. Home Feed – shows what the people you're following are saying.

2. Text field – where you enter in the text you want to include in your tweet.

3. Mentions – shows people who have mentioned you using the @ symbol.

4. Direct Messages – shows messages sent privately to you.

5 & 6. Your Accounts – HootSuite allows you to monitor and post to multiple Twitter, Facebook and Linked-In accounts.

7. Replies – shows everyone that has replied to your tweets.

By default Hootsuite starts with the following columns in the second tab:
1. The replies column.
2. Your whole stream of Twitter followers.
3. Tweets that have been scheduled but not yet sent.
4. Messages sent directly to you are the columns shown.

The first tab contains a "featured" column. I suggest clicking the x on the first tab to close it. You'll never open it or want to recreate it. Trust me. It contains the HootSuite Twitter account and some others that HootSuite thinks are fun to follow. Don't get sucked into looking at this for even a little while, as it's sure to distract you from what's most important.

Place the tabs in this order, which you can do by clicking and dragging them:
• Home Feed
• Mentions
• Direct Messages (to you)
• Replies
• Followers
• Pending Messages (messages you have queued up for later but not yet sent, empty for now)

Close any other open tabs. Now, type the name of your restaurant in the search box, and save this as a column. If your restaurant name is hard to spell, add variations of the spelling as well. If there are multiple words in your restaurant's name, add those words with a space between them and in quotation marks (for AJ Bombers, you'd type in "AJ Bombers") to make sure you can monitor these as well.

Add another column for any unique menu items (2 maximum) that you have and hope people will be talking about. This should give you a maximum of ten columns. If you have more than 10 columns, you won't be able to get through this in just 30 minutes, plus HootSuite will make you use another tab. Trust me, 10 columns is PLENTY to watch. Here's another tool we suggest: A kitchen timer that goes up to 30 minutes.

You need to be disciplined to make this work. You could easily spend an hour or more on this solution, as you'll get lost in the stream and feel the need to get it all done. With Twitter, it's never "all done" so let this utopia idea go. Focus on just 30 minutes a day, and you can make Twitter a solid part of your business.

Now let's get to work on the actual solution.

First, set your kitchen timer to 30 minutes, no more, no less.
Go to http://hootsuite.com - Log into HootSuite.

Step 1:
Look at the first column you have set up: Mentions. Respond to anyone who mentions you. If you do nothing else every day, you should respond to everyone who mentions you personally. If someone took the time to mention you, they likely are already customers or folks who want to get to know you better so they can become customers.

NOTE: If you get any complaints in your overnight stream, make sure you take care of these FIRST. (Make sure you read the upcoming chapter about service recovery so you know how to respond to complaints.)

Now, scroll to the bottom of the column from where you last responded, and go up from there. If you don't think you can get through responding to everyone personally, include 3 or 4 Twitter handles (@username) in a message and say thank you to them. If they ask you a question, respond with the answer, or respond with your phone number so they can call to speak with you directly.

You can respond by mousing over the tweet, and clicking on the reply button. A quick "Thanks for your business" is enough. Joe sometimes re-tweets their message and adds a quick "thanks" at the end of the message. Find your style and use it. You do NOT need to respond to everyone who says, "Thanks for the RT," or anything like that that doesn't seem personal.

You may never get beyond this step, and that's okay on days when you only have 30 minutes to work with Twitter. On days you have more time, take more time.

By the way, when you're first starting out on Twitter, you'll seldom have ANYONE mention you directly because they won't know your Twitter handle. Don't get discouraged. Just like your business didn't get built in a day, neither will your Twitter followers.

Step 2:
Respond to direct messages. These are messages from people you are following, but wanted to ask you a question or leave you a comment in private. Some of these will be automatic because you followed someone. Don't waste your 30 minutes with anything that isn't a question or comment about your business.

Step 3:
Look at your stream and see if there's anything happening locally that you can show your support for. Click on the re-tweet button to share it with your stream, and get it out to your followers. I recommend sharing no more than 5 of these a day if you're using our 30-Minute Twitter Solution.

Step 4:
Look at your column for restaurant mentions. Quickly handle any complaints using our chapter on service recovery as a guide and say thank you for anyone who said nice things.

Step 5:
Look at your column for mentions of your menu items. Quickly handle any complaints using our chapter on service recovery as a guide and say thank you for anyone who said nice things.

Step 6:
Schedule a note for later about your breakfast/lunch/happy hour/dinner specials for the rest of the week. This can be done using the "schedule

for later" feature in the HootSuite window. We recommend scheduling at least an hour in advance of the time you want customers to arrive at your establishment to give them time to plan their next move, but not too long so they forget about you. Schedule these for the top of the hour.

Step 7:
Schedule for later a "link" or a comment about something of interest one of your customers or someone in your neighborhood did or is doing during each day that week, if possible. Include their Twitter handle if you have it. Schedule these for the bottom of the hour.

Scheduling these two items at the top and the bottom of the hour will give them time between so folks don't get overwhelmed by what you're saying. Few people want constant Twitter chatter so a few tweets like this a day will be plenty.

Step 8:
Re-tweet some more of the worthy tweets from the folks you're following.

Step 9:
Go to the column mentioning your restaurant and your menu items; follow anyone who has mentioned you that you aren't currently following.

Step 10:
With any remaining time, start over and do it all again.

Notes:

#TwitterWorks – When time is scarce, you need a plan for using Twitter. The 30-Minute Twitter Solution offers a plan for maximizing your time by connecting first with those who talk to and about your business.

#TwitterWorks

10 commandments of social media for your employees.

We know how incredibly busy — make that crazy — the food service industry can be. In fact, you're probably wondering how you're ever going to find the time to even attempt using Twitter. But there's no reason you have to do it all yourself! You have a staff that you can utilize. And chances are, your staff is probably more familiar with Twitter than you are. Just as your restaurant has a system for delivering food, you need a system for delivering social media. It's very important to take the time to build a great system that you can hand off to your staff. This involves training and establishing guidelines for your employees before you allow them to tweet away. We suggest employing these 10 Commandments of Social Media to ensure you are comfortable and confident that your staff will reflect positively on your business.

1. Customer face-to-face always comes first. When you're in the restaurant, always focus on the customers in front of you first. Head down into your mobile device or computer is always second to the customer standing in front of you.

2. Never say negative things about a restaurant group, other restaurants, employees, customers or anyone on Twitter. Saying negative things can have an adverse affect on everyone in your establishment.

3. Spelling counts. Take the time to spell things correctly. It makes you look more professional and shows that you care about the little things, which will reflect positively on your restaurant.

4. No swearing. Nothing looks less professional than cursing online. If you wouldn't say it in front of your grandmother, don't say it at all.

5. Respond to all messages in public. If someone mentions you – good, bad or otherwise – make an effort to at least say thank you for the mention.

6. Service recovery starts in public, gets taken care of in private, and then is shared in public. Anyone who complains about anything should be acknowledged as soon as possible. Follow them immediately. Send a public message to invite them to send you a direct message with their phone number, or share your phone number so you can talk to them privately and understand the problem. Fix the problem promptly if you can, or share an expectation of when it will be fixed. Say thanks for the opportunity to fix things in public.

According to Nielsen, over 50% of people will have smart phones by 2011 enabling them to share their dining experience with videos and photos instantly.

7. Follow back any non-spammer. If someone seeks you out on Twitter and follows you to see what you say – and they aren't spammers – follow them back. This allows them to direct message you, and makes them feel closer to you and that their words matter.

8. You must disclose your relationship to the restaurant. Don't hide the fact you work where you do. Disclose this on your bio page, or whenever you say nice things about the restaurant.

9. Bring any customer or non-customer complaints to a manager. If someone says something negative about the restaurant, let your manager know. It may be nothing, but to the person complaining, it may be EVERYTHING. And, they may bring it up the next time they try your goods so it's best to give the manager a heads up.

10. If you're not sure what you should do, always ask for help from your manager. You're going to encounter things you've never seen before. You don't have to handle them alone. Ask for help if you're not sure…after you acknowledge the problem.

Notes:

#TwitterWorks – Set some guidelines for your employees' use of Twitter. Help them know what's right and wrong. Tweak things to make them fit YOUR style, but please, set SOME guidelines. In the absence of knowledge, folks will make up their own stories and handle things as they see fit…and this may not be in the best interest of your restaurant.

#TwitterWorks

A little more about our stories.

Success – It's not all on purpose (by @ajbombers)

So much of what happened over the past year has been what I would call a "happy accident." By that I mean I didn't set out to make several thousand new friends/followers on Twitter. I was just playing around and trying to figure out if this Twitter thing might bring in a few more customers by connecting with folks around the city of Milwaukee.

I found a guest talking about her experience. This guest had tweeted that she had thoroughly enjoyed herself the night before at Swig, another of my restaurants in Milwaukee. I replied with not much more than a simple thank you for her business – and within minutes, she had rebroadcast (RT'd) my thank you to her personal Twitter world of 400 of her "friends" about what a great meal she had at one of our restaurants. Many of her friends then decided to follow Swig on Twitter.

This opened my eyes to the potential business application of social media. I realized we were onto something that could be great for our group of businesses, since we were really trying hard to foster this sort of personal connection. Guests could speak directly with me about their experiences and thoughts about our restaurants.

Joe Sorge standing on a table next to one of the famous P-Nut drop zones at AJ Bombers.

Steve Mai and Scott Baitinger standing in front of the Milwaukee Public Market and the Streetza Truck.

It seemed this medium was created to perfectly complement our company's overall marketing strategy of permission-style marketing, as opposed to the traditional style of interruption marketing that most companies employ.

Since then, Twitter has brought in many more customers; gotten my restaurants mentioned in the Wall Street Journal, the NY Times, on CNN, Hubspot.com, Nations Restaurant News, featured on The Travel Channel's Food Wars and in blogs and websites around the world. More importantly, it has lead to some wonderful friendships.

One of the newest burgers at AJ Bombers, the Sham Wow, created by Jeremy of Flux Design.

It's about more than just pizza and Twitter (by @streetzapizza)

My goal with Twitter was first to build brand stewards, some customer evangelists, and yes, a few friendships. The first page of the Streetza business plan states: We will not use traditional paid media to build this brand. As a person who spends 40-50 hours a week developing advertising, this was a pretty far departure from my norm.

When we created Streetza, one of the things we wanted to do was share our love of pizza with people. This love would manifest itself into our food. And to ensure that people would love our pizza, we asked them to help create not only the pizza, but also every aspect of our business.

First, we invited people we already had relationships with to help us build Streetza. Via Facebook and Myspace, we asked them which name they liked best for the concept. We had them review 12 different logos we had created, and ultimately select the one that would be placed on all of our materials. While we were still in the early stages, and testing different crusts and sauces, we invited them to my garage, where we had hooked up our first Blodgett oven. We made 30-40 different types of pizza and listened to what they liked and didn't like; and then we altered our pizza to reflect their insights.

And that was before we signed up for Twitter.

Our first tweet came on May 1, 2009. I stayed up late one night and decided to take the leap into Twitter. I had read many of the blog posts from social media experts, like Chris Brogan, Gary Vaynerchuk and others. By following their advice and using the tools they suggested, I began monitoring conversations as they were happening. The first thing I typed into the search bar of Twitter was "pizza." You would not believe the number of results that came back. Thousands of people were talking about pizza on Twitter. The next thing I entered was "Milwaukee." Once again, thousands of conversations were going on about Milwaukee. It was also here that I first located people in Milwaukee using Twitter.

A Twitter tip: Attend or host a tweetup. It's an event where people who Twitter come together to meet in person. Some tweetups are purely social, others are focused on raising money for a charity.

I wrote an article for Magazine SOHO in June 2009, in which I used a cocktail party as an analogy for using social media. For some people, the thought of dropping into a cocktail party, where they don't know anyone, is frightening. That is exactly what your first impression of Twitter may be. Here is a room full of people who have relationships with each other. How do I introduce myself to people and start talking to them? One idea is to first assess what you do know. This is a cocktail party for "_____", being put on by "_____". This will at least give you some idea of the type of people who are at the party, perhaps a glimpse into what their interests are, and who at the party could potentially introduce you to others. When many businesses start tweeting, they act like an annoying sales person at that cocktail party. Running around the room with their business cards and trying to sell their wares to everyone there. That usually leads to not being invited back to the next party. Rather than doing that, walk around the room, get to know people and interact with them naturally.

This is what we did when we started tweeting. I found some people from Milwaukee on Twitter and started interacting with them. Some of the first people were: @jonkurozawa, who I later learned was married to a woman I went to grade school and high school with; @Pezzettino, who is a talented and visionary musician in Milwaukee; and @spreenkler, who I knew of from the Milwaukee advertising world, but really hadn't talked with until we started interacting on Twitter. And @bflay. Yes, Bobby Flay, the celebrity chef! On the second day we were on Twitter, we were talking to one of the most famous and well-respected chefs in the world.

One of the main parts of our social media strategy was to locate journalists on Twitter, and hopefully interact with them. Within a week, we were having conversations with @NewsHub, the main Twitter account from The Milwaukee Journal Sentinel, @OnMilwaukee, the largest local online publication, @BlatzLiquor, one the most active businesses on Twitter in Milwaukee, and @milwaukeefoodie, one of the most popular local food blogs. We also started having conversations with @Pogue. David Pogue is the Technology Columnist from the NY Times. David was looking for @ replies to some questions for a book he was working on. I replied to a question about how people had proposed marriage. I responded and my tweet was selected for his book. "The World According to Twitter."

A quick re-cap. After one week: We had 300 followers, including key local media, who were actively listening to the story of how we were building a pizza truck. We interacted with other local businesses that advised us on everything from accounting and point-of-sale systems, to where we should park our trucks so we could find lots of people. We talked with Bobby Flay, a world famous chef, and our tweet was included in a book by NY Times best-selling author David Pogue.

In the weeks following, Twitter worked for us in ways we couldn't have ever imagined. While we had a strategy in place, there have been so many aspects that we never planned on. Some of the most memorable and important things that have happened in the following weeks include:

- **The first night that the Streetza truck hit the street,** over 720 people came to visit and try a slice. People I had never met before were coming up to the truck at each location telling us they followed us on Twitter, and how they were looking forward to meeting us and trying our pizza.

- **About two weeks after opening,** our truck experienced electrical problems. We asked our Twitter followers if they knew of anyone who was a large truck mechanic. Within one hour, someone from Twitter had sent over their mechanic friend to help us fix the problem.

- **After our 5th week on Twitter,** I attended a Milwaukee Interactive Marketing Association meeting about Twitter. A public discussion started about people using Twitter in interesting ways. Both @streetzapizza and @BlatzLiquor were mentioned. At this meeting, I had not yet identified myself as being @streetzapizza. It was really great to hear firsthand what people liked and what they found helpful.

- **Around Week 6,** our Twitter followers told us about a festival called "Chill on the Hill" and invited us to attend. This festival was one of the most rewarding, profitable and fun venues that Streetza has served.

- **On Week 7,** we found out about the WISN A-list, a consumer-driven survey in which all of Milwaukee votes on their favorite things, such as restaurants, wedding photographers, pizza, etc. We applied to be a part of the competition, but were initially denied entry because as a food truck, we didn't have a physical location (a requirement for the pizza category.) We asked our Twitter followers to tell WISN that this wasn't fair. It worked, and we were allowed into the competition. After over 57,000 people had voted, Streetza ended up winning 2nd Best Pizza in the city.

- **Week 8,** we received a really interesting tweet from a follower. Apparently we had been named by Jalopnik.com as one of the 10 Best Food Trucks. Awesome! I had never heard of this site. It's a site entirely dedicated to automotive culture, reviews and lifestyle. They found out about us on Twitter and thought we had a neat concept. They wrote a story about us based on our tweets, looked at what people were saying about us in their tweets, and determined that we must have pretty darn good food. The article has had 38,000 views, 82 comments and has been shared hundreds of times on Facebook, Digg and through tweets.

- **Week 8 through Week 50,** the number of things that happened to us because of our Twitter activity is unbelievable. We were named one of the 10 Best Food Trucks in the U.S. by GQ Magazine. We have been featured in Time Magazine, Men.Style.com, ESPN.com, MS-NBC.com, The Onion, on John Tesh's nationally-syndicated radio show, and in hundreds and hundreds of local and national articles. We've been featured on NBC Nightly News with Brian Williams, WTMJ 4, a NBC station, Fox 6, the local Fox Station, and on Food Reporter, an internet video show hosted by Karen Cooks It. We've spoken to people from the Travel Channel, the Food Network and the Cooking Channel. We talked to some of Rachael Ray's people, Anthony Bourdain's people and many others.

• **On Week 51,** we were preparing to exibit and speak at the National Restaurant Association Show in Chicago and decided to redesign the truck. Rather than choosing our final design ourselves, we wanted to include the people who had helped to make us successful. Three design options were posted on our website. We asked people to vote, post comments and help guide us. 780 people voted in less than one week and 4,200 people visited the "Streetza 2.0 Truck Design" page on our site.

A Twitter tip: get people involved! Let them vote on menu items, restaurant decor, special offers or anything else you can dream up.

We launched the Streetza 2.0 truck live on television during the Fox 6 Wake Up News.

Twitter is not only a great way to communicate with your customers – it's a great way to co mmunicate with the media. According to PR Newswire, the global leader in innovative communications and marketing services, "In both the US and Canada, PR pitches through a social network resulted in coverage approximately 70% of the time. In contrast, the standard pitch to a US or Canadian journalist rarely leads to coverage, with 66% pegging the success rate at 0-20%."

AJ Bombers used Twitter to target and communicate with the Travel Channel show.

As a result of that targeted effort, the Travel Channel came to Milwaukee to film an episode and many AJ Bombers fans came to support the restaurant.

Those are pretty powerful numbers. Now, this doesn't mean you don't need a PR firm or an ad agency. One of the reasons social media has worked so well for us is that we have used it strategically. By day, I am a creative director at an advertising agency, which develops strategy and creative executions of those strategies for many different types of clients.

That being said, even if you don't have the budget to hire an ad agency or a PR firm, you can still accomplish just as much as a large restaurant chain with hundreds of thousands of dollars at their disposal.

Seth Godin characterizes the process of the dynamics of Social Media Content Strategy this way:

Here's what we used to do:

Create —> Edit —> Launch

Here's what happens now:

Create —> Launch —> Edit —> Launch —> Repeat

Social media offers a fantastic opportunity for the restaurant. It allows you to create and launch media properties directly to the public. But even more of a blessing is the direct and indirect feedback process that naturally happens in this space.

You put something out there and the crowd will reveal the direction you should go. It's not necessarily always the wisdom of the crowd, but rather the desires and objections of the crowd that guide you. It consistently amazes me that a food truck, open only 10 hours a week, is able to stay top of mind throughout the week by thousands of people I've interacted with on Twitter.

A Happy Accident (by @philgerb)

I may not own a restaurant, but I love food and the restaurant industry. Growing up in a town of 996 people (Crivitz, Wisconsin, to be exact), I worked at a supper club as a waiter, cook and dishwasher, and loved it all. I loved the food and I loved the people – including those I worked with and the customers I worked for.

In a small town, word of mouth is critical to the success of a business. One customer can make or break, a restaurant. Thankfully, people loved the restaurant where I worked and we were relatively successful. I not only left Crivitz but actually left Wisconsin and the restaurant industry altogether, when I joined the Navy after graduating from high school. But I never stopped enjoying great food and great service by great people.

In 1996, I moved back to Wisconsin, to the city of Milwaukee. Milwaukee is a relatively small town, too. Though we have 330,000 people, everyone in Milwaukee knows each other. Word of mouth, and a little "word of mouse" with OnMilwaukee.com, was the only way things got around… until recently.

Enter Twitter.

Twitter allows me to connect with food fanatics around the city and find out what they love about a particular restaurant. I can send out a quick tweet of "Know any great burger places in downtown Milwaukee?" and get an answer back in a hurry.

This is how I met @ajbombers (my co-author and now friend, Joe Sorge). Joe heard my cry for great burgers and invited me into his restaurant. He also began following me on Twitter to learn who I was and what I was all about.

When I went into his restaurant the first few times, he wasn't even there. I know because when I tweeted him that I was coming, and he tweeted me right back to let me know he wasn't there. but to ask for Mike, and Mike would take care of me.

As I was leaving AJ Bombers the first time, I sent a tweet out thanking @ajbombers for the service and the good food (I didn't even know his name) and he sent me a tweet right back thanking me for my business.

A very excited Phil Gerbyshak wins a prize at the first annual AJ Bombers, Streetza Pizza and Blatz Liquor halloween party.

Though it took 3 or 4 tries to finally meet Joe, when I did, he recognized me right away from my Twitter avatar, and came up to shake my hand. We found out we shared a love for restaurants and marketing, and quickly became friends.

I met Scott in a similar way. I saw this guy sharing his thoughts about Milwaukee, pizza and other topics in a clear, concise way, and interacting with those that interacted with him.

Curious for more, I had to see this cool pizza truck and meet the man behind the tweets. While I was speaking at a conference while Scott was there with his pizza truck, and made time to connect with me a bit in person between the 100 other hungry patrons he had to serve.

The most fun part however, was what happened AFTER the event: Scott took the time to reconnect with me on Twitter and we started talking about the events of the day. We shared some insights, swapped stories, and agreed to stay in touch.

A few months later, the idea for this book was launched...and the rest is history.

Twitter Makes Partnerships Possible

Before I started using Twitter, I'd never been to AJ Bombers. I'd never had a Streetza pizza. As a matter of fact, I'd never heard of either place. And I'd never met either of my co-authors, Joe and Scott.

But then Twitter happened to Joe and Scott. They started tweeting at me. I started tweeting at them. We started a conversation, and (dare I say) a relationship, before we ever met each other live.

We got to learn each other's interests by reading through each other's tweets, by following links we shared, by asking questions, by interacting frequently on Twitter and letting things develop naturally.

I learned Joe owned several restaurants in the Milwaukee area and, like me, he was fascinated by social media – not for the tools or the numbers, but for the relative ease at which you can connect with just about anybody if only you'll put it out there and try to connect to them.

Joe Sorge, Scott Baitinger and Phil Gerbyshak tweeting.

Scott was a little easier to befriend. I met Scott working inside his pizza truck after following him for several months on Twitter. We chatted a little bit about how and why he was using Twitter, and what results he was seeing. We connected again at a holiday party at (where else?) AJ Bombers. We laughed a lot, shared some pictures and some funny stories, and quickly realized we were cut from the same cloth of loving people and being very intrigued about social media.

Now some six months later, I'm fortunate enough to call AJ Bombers and Streetza Pizza two of my favorite places to enjoy dinner, hang out and share with my friends. And I'm even MORE fortunate to call Joe and Scott my friends; guys I enjoy spending time with even when we're not talking about the book you're reading.

Karen Gill, @karencooksit at the Milwaukee Tweetup holiday party.

The 2009 Milwaukee Holiday Tweetup Party.

#TwitterWorks – You can learn who your REAL customers are by using Twitter. Cater to them by catering to their kids, and you'll be selling more cat (and restaurant) food than ever before.

#TwitterWorks

A truck is just a vehicle. Pizza is just food.

The truck is just a vehicle. Our pizza is just pizza. Neither have any personality, and neither are really that interesting. From the get-go I knew that if I wanted to engage with people and have them think highly of us, we needed to be transparent, entertaining and informative. We tweet more about other things happening in the city than we actually tweet about our pizza.

In large markets, such as Los Angeles and New York, tens of thousands of people follow food trucks like @KogiBBQ and @Waffletruck. In the first weeks of using social media, I realized that what we were going to do, and how we would do it, would be very different than these other twittering food trucks. If you look at their Twitter accounts, you'll find it a constant stream of advertising and listings of where they are serving. They have thousands of followers, yet only a few hundred people they follow back. I've felt from the beginning that if someone is willing to listen to what I have to say, I should at the very least listen to what they are talking about.

Our goal was to build brand awareness for Streetza. We wanted to first find our target market and gather followers in it. Five people who will actually do business with you can be far more valuable than 500 who aren't that engaged. In our case, we identified different target audiences:

While photos of us making pizza are exciting to us, to really engage with people, we try to take shots of people who are participating and sharing the pizza and the Streetza experience.

1. **People in Milwaukee.**

2. **Local and national journalists.**

3. **People interested in food.**

4. **People interested in social media.**

5. **People who would potentially be interested in developing a partnership with us to bring Streetza to additional markets.**

If you look at our Twitter account, you'll find that we try to keep conversations going with all of these groups throughout the week. And with each audience, we try to do the following things*:

1. **Create demand.** We try to communicate just how delicious our product is in an interesting and compelling way.

2. **Humanize Streetza.** We reveal ourselves through our tweets, our flaws and our triumphs. I was the first to admit on Twitter that "pizza testing" resulted in me gaining 30 pounds over the course of the past year. People connect with people. Be yourself when you tweet and you can build much stronger relationships with your followers.

3. **Gather feedback.** We've listened to our followers from day one. And we've followed their suggestions. Our menu has changed to incorporate other people's suggestions. We've added different topping choices and daily specials, a gluten-free option, and we even created a pizza line called the #fitmke pizzas. We noticed a community being formed around a hashtag in Milwaukee. The #fitmke group was started by @ Bananza, @tmgessner and @BrennanMKE. The group is dedicated to

---

* We followed someone else's advice when we started. This plan is loosely based on the Mashable article "Tweetable Eats: What Street Vendors can Teach Businesses About Twitter." – Ann Handley – You can read the full article at http://mashable.com/2009/07/17/twitter-street-vendors/

promoting and providing healthy and fun activities in Milwaukee. Admittedly, pizza is rarely thought of as a healthy food. But we spent 8 weeks researching how to make a delicious low-calorie version of Streetza. It ended up being one of our most popular menu items. We have pizzas that have only 155 calories per slice, yet are topped with loads of veggies and chicken-based sausages. Everything about how, when and where we operate has influenced our menu.

4. **Run fun and relevant promotions.** We've given away concert tickets, food, gift cards, autographed stuff and a chance to meet celebrity chefs throughout the past year. For instance, when we learned that Anthony Bourdain was coming to town, we thought "What better way to get the Travel Channel producers to notice us than to have our followers point us out to them?!" We purchased two front-row tickets to see Tony while he was in Milwaukee. For an entire week, we asked people to re-tweet things about Tony's show "No Reservations." Each re-tweet was an entry into the drawing. There were over 1500 entries, which meant there were 1500 tweets in a week, talking about us and Tony Bourdain in the same 140 characters. This resulted in tweets and a call from the Travel Channel so that they could find out just who this "Streetza" was.

5. **Create a sense of community or join in one.** If you've never heard of a tweet-up, don't worry…neither had we 12 months ago. One of the most intimidating aspects of Twitter for many is the step that involves engaging with people. How do I get people to engage with us? Why are people going to care about what I have to say? One of the easiest ways to start engaging with people is to simply join them in what they are already doing. About three weeks after we started tweeting, we noticed that everyone in the community was going to be attending a tweet-up. What is a tweet-up? It's basically an event created around people using Twitter. There are many different types of tweet-ups. Some are purely social, some help to raise funds for different charities and some are hosted by local businesses. Tweet-ups allow people who interact with each other on Twitter to meet and interact in person. One of the most powerful things about social media is the ability to interact with people outside of

it as well as inside of it. We volunteered to bring pizza to a tweet-up being held at @BlatzLiquor, and sponsored by @NewsHub. This was pretty much a no-brainer: The most popular guy on Twitter and the most powerful local media outlet were having a party. We could not only invite ourselves, we could allow all of these people to try our food. Before the event even started, we saw people on Twitter talking about how they were excited to try our pizza. We got the chance to meet lots of people and humanize Streetza even more. One week later, the Milwaukee Journal Sentinel ran a story about a food truck that was using Twitter – us.

As time progressed, we started having our own tweet-ups. We also shared events that we attended with people. While I am trained as an art director, I am not a photographer and you probably aren't either. Still, you can purchase a nice camera to capture what you are doing. Pretending you are a photographer is a good idea. You never know who or how many people will look at the events you capture. In less than one year, the Streetza Flickr account has had 68,000 people look at our photos.

8,942 people looked at the photos from A Streetza Halloween on Flickr. 3,300 of them on the day we posted them.

Out on the town

WHS SLIDE SHOW INFO

Photo Posted: Sep. 14, 2009

Photo 3 of 40

Go to Grid View

JSOnline
JOURNAL SENTINEL

The photos we took at the Wisconsin Humane Society's anniversary party even ended up in the Milwaukee Journal / Sentinel online photo gallery.

Once again, it's not just about pizza. No one would look at photos of pizza more than once. We photograph the events we're attending in what we feel is an interesting way. For instance, when we were at the Wisconsin Humane Society's anniversary party, I walked around when the pizza truck wasn't busy and shot photos of people's dogs – from the dogs' level. Our collection of dog's eye photos were viewed 8,000 times on our Flickr page, and picked up by local publications. Thanks to some creative staging, the Streetza truck was usually positioned somewhere in the background.

6. **Integrate.** Twitter is only one of the social media tools available. Identifying where your target audience is was the first thing mentioned in this chapter. Streetza uses Twitter, flickr, YouTube, Linked-in, Facebook, Wordpress, Ning, Foursquare and Gowalla. Like any marketing plan, social media works best when you integrate your efforts in different mediums.

Putting guests to work for charity.

Our guest bartending/chef program at AJBombers allows us to put our guests in control of a promotion, while raise money for a cause or charity that is near and dear to them personally. We've helped our guests raise money for The Milwaukee Rescue Mission, The Crohns and Colitis Foundation, The Blood Center of Wisconsin, The MS Society, Fallen and Injured US Soldiers, Education and Scholastic funds, and certain memorial funds, like The Sharon Iggulden Memorial Fund. We've even used guest bartending activities to send our local Social Media Community in Milwaukee to South by SouthWest, a set of interactive, film, and music festivals and conferences that take place every spring in Austin, Texas. We even raised money to send one of our guests to Denmark for a semester overseas.

It feels great to give our guests a platform to raise awareness and funds for their causes, via our restaurants, and we'd allow them to do so everyday if we could. In the end, our guest bartending/chef program is also just good business. After all, it's our job to make our guests happy in any and everyway possible.

Use non-traditional media to attract traditional media coverage.

Where else can you interact instantly with a celebrity, an influential person in the media, or a customer within a minute of each other? Without Twitter, there is no way major media, such as The Travel Channel, MSNBC, TIME Magazine, GQ Magazine or VendrTV, would have known we exist. No way we could have had conversations with people like Gordon Ramsey, Bobby Flay, Chris Brogan, or David Pogue. Google has a lot of great information, but I'm pretty sure it would be difficult to find contacts of this caliber – and near impossible to have them listen to what you have to say.

Celebrities and the media use Twitter for the same reason you should – to interact with people, learn about new cool things and share your viewpoint and stories. So the ones who are using it correctly are listening.

As mentioned in previous chapters, we wanted Anthony Bourdain to be aware of us prior to his visit to Milwaukee. By holding a little contest that cost us almost nothing, we had 1500 people tell The Travel Channel about us. They re-tweeted information about our contest to 70,000+ of their followers, resulting in us gaining 300+ new followers. We also had a call later that day from a production company. And, when Tony came to town, he already knew who we were, and we had the opportunity to share our story with him. We also got him to autograph a bunch of items, which we shared with our Twitter followers.

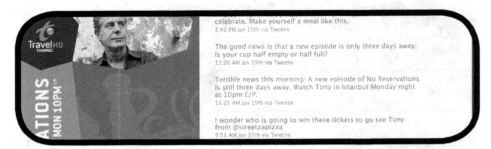

The Travel Channel's show, No Reservations starring Anthony Bourdain has 90,000 Twitter followers. Those 90,000 people saw Streetza Pizza's name for almost 2 hours. Twitter also was how GQ, TIME and Inc. Magazine learned about Streetza.

What happens when the spotlight turns on you?

Here's where the story took an interesting turn for our business at AJ Bombers: I thought Chris Brogan was at home in Boston, sending out a tweet announcing, "Hey Milwaukee, here I come." In response, I tweeted, "If you're looking for sustenance, check out @ajbombers @swigmilwaukee @water_buffalo."

Unbeknown to me, Chris was right around the corner at another local establishment. Chris sent me a private message, asking me not to share this with anyone and we decided to get together.

We shook hands, cracked open a few beers and I started telling him the story about @ajbombers. Suddenly, Chris stopped me, pulled out his video camera and started recording me. "Who are you and what's YOUR story?" asked Chris. So, I told my story of a restaurant built by Twitter. Chris videotaped for a few minutes, posted it on his site, and turned it into one of his famed "Kitchen Table Talks."

The next day, Chris was named the #1 Social Media Expert by Social Media Explorer, and my interview was on the front page of his site. This made a lot of people interested in our story. It also turned into several feature articles (blog posts), more interviews and all sorts of other cool things. When Chris arrived in Milwaukee, I treated him the same way I would treat anyone. Nobody else had reached out to him. The mere act of reaching out in an authentic way brought Chris into our restaurant. We'd been using social media long before Chris Brogan came around. Now, I find myself using social media in ways beyond the style that I've always employed; more strategically, I'd even say.

The video that Chris Brogan made about AJ Bombers has been watched, tweeted and blogged about thousands of times.

Engagement at the point of experience.

The style of service that our restaurant company provides and the overall guest service promise, lends to the efficient use of social media tools. I can treat you the same way in this new public domain as I would treat you, live and in-person, inside one of our locations.

When you tell me you're there, I can thank you for coming. I can share some suggestions of what to try on the menu. And, I can tell you who at my restaurant will give you the best treatment in the house. This builds trust and relationships…if you deliver the goods!

It's very unique to the hospitality industry. I have the opportunity to connect with you on a personal level and treat you as the most special person in the world.

And if I decide not to send it via direct message to just you, other guests on Twitter (followers) can see how I treat my guests, and will crave that level of service, too.

I tell people, "If you want me to really prove it, follow me OR visit my restaurant." When people come into your restaurant and tweet about their experience, they will expect you to respond or at least acknowledge that you're listening.

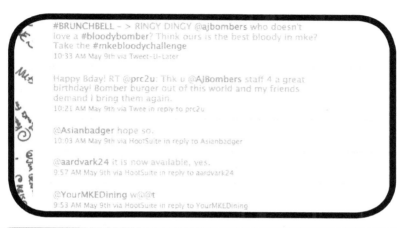

#BRUNCHBELL – > RINGY DINGY @ajbombers who doesn't love a #bloodybomber? Think ours is the best bloody in mke? Take the #mkebloodychallenge
10:33 AM May 9th via Tweet-U-Later

Happy Bday! RT @prc2u: Thk u @AJBombers staff 4 a great birthday! Bomber burger out of this world and my friends demand I bring them again.
10:21 AM May 9th via Twee in reply to prc2u

@Asianbadger hope so.
10:03 AM May 9th via HootSuite in reply to Asianbadger

@aardvark24 it is now available, yes.
9:57 AM May 9th via HootSuite in reply to aardvark24

@YourMKEDining w@@t
9:53 AM May 9th via HootSuite in reply to YourMKEDining

Twitter lets you engage with people whether you are at your restaurant or not.

People expect an immediate (or sooner) response.

Think about your business: If someone calls or e-mails you for a reservation for dinner, can you wait 3 days to respond? Can you wait 3 hours? 3 minutes? Everyone has a tolerance for how long is too long, so try to respond as quickly as possible.

Joe is awesome at responding to messages quickly, whether via direct message or a mention in a tweet. In just one year of business at AJ Bombers, Joe has sent over twelve thousand public tweets, with no doubt thousands of private (direct) messages.

Joe responds to tweets around the clock, and his customers expect it. When asked if he can keep it up, he'll smile and respond, "As long as I can do it, I will. My customers expect it."

When you look at AJBombers on twitter, you'll instantly see that responses are instant, authentic and personal. This is how you build relationships that last.

Keep your message as authentic as your ingredients.

Automation makes you less credible and less YOU. It scares people into thinking it isn't a real person behind the message, but rather a machine programmed to spew out nice stuff. People want to connect with real people, not with a robot. They want to connect with an authentic person, someone who is LIKE THEM, someone who will be at the restaurant when they show up.

It doesn't have to be the owner. It can be a bartender, a waitress, the cook. Anyone. But it has to be someone.

Not an automated message.

None of us use automatic direct messages when folks follow us. Many people we've followed in the past do. Phil has his Twitter account set up to block anyone who has an automated follow message.

Don't get us wrong, some automation is good, such as scheduling your tweets via a tool. @ajbombers sends out scheduled messages for the lunch bell to get people's attention. They've actually become a moniker of who the restaurant is, and customers ask about it when we don't do it.

@philgerb schedules programmed tweets during the day to avoid excessively posting tweets in a short period of time.

But make no mistake, full automation does NOT work. Full automation isn't real, and it isn't authentic.

If you think a machine can do this by picking up keywords and mentions, and sending out an automated "thank you," you're sorely mistaken. People need and CRAVE human interaction with the places they do business.

Notes:

#TwitterWorks – Remember you're doing all this in front of an audience, so customers can learn your restaurant is great about fixing problems WITHOUT them personally having to experience the error. Take time to seek out these bad experiences and admit you have screwed up...in public.

#TwitterWorks

Give it away – and it will come back to you.

When the truck first rolled out onto Milwaukee's streets, we were met with some serious opposition from traditional brick and mortar businesses. The first night, we planned to drive around town and simply give away pizza to help build some excitement and awareness about Streetza. We were asked to leave several times by the businesses we parked in front of.

While Milwaukee city code allows us to park in front of any business we want, we choose to only park in front of businesses that offer nothing that would be considered direct competition. For us, parking in front of a bar or boutique is okay, but parking in front of another restaurant is not something we would ever do.

Nevertheless, initially those bars and boutiques really didn't want us in front of their business. We changed their opinion 180 degrees, to the point where now lots of businesses invite us to park in front of them, and ask us to serve our food inside of their building or collaborate on marketing initiatives with them.

To do this, we needed to change people's perception of street food in Milwaukee. When we hit the streets, the only street food Milwaukee really had was hot dog carts. The gourmet food cart movement that was sweeping LA hadn't reached Milwaukee yet. We were really the first to elevate street food in the city. We did that by partnering with our customers, the media and anyone else who shared our values, love of food or other common interests.

We donated pizzas and a percentage of our profits to other organizations, such as WMSE (a local listener-supported radio station), The Milwaukee Hurling Club, The Bay View Historical Society, The National MS Society, The Milwaukee VA Hospital, The Humane Society and many others. And we invited our friends on Twitter to help us help others. We served as a collection point for the local Fox station's Coats For Kids Program. We collected and matched DVD donations for the Veteran's Association, and we even partnered with rapper JC Poppe to raise money through a special meal that included a slice of pizza, a soda and his latest CD.

We invited local artists to exhibit their artwork on our truck during Milwaukee's Gallery Night. As a part-time instructor at MIAD, Milwaukee's 4-year college of art and design, I know how difficult it can be for young artists to find space to exhibit in a gallery. We invited them to present their work on our truck, which was parked alongside some of Milwaukee's best galleries. The amount of attention they received was amazing. All fun. All interesting. All sharing with very deserving people. And all tweeted about by our followers.

Our "Art on a Truck" night resulted in record setting sales, media coverage and 3,500 views of photos from the night.

The return of the Sunday Family Dinner.

Water Buffalo restaurant is a three-year-old restaurant. In November of 2009, we were doing our first major updating of the menu. I (Joe) was thinking of how to expose people to this new menu, and was reading the book, "Viral Loop."

I thought to myself, "Let's combine the transparency and authenticity of what social media can be, expose our customers to our new menu and let our customers tell us what they think of the new items. I'll encourage them to take some pictures of the food, share it with their friends and ask the chef and me questions."

And so, the #wbtastetweet was born.

We invited some of our closest Twitter friends from our other restaurants to try new menu items. These were folks already in our inner circle of trust, who we weren't afraid we would be dragging away from our other restaurants. We chose the safest group – and the most honest group. We sat down and ordered the new featured drinks, sampled some new wine, shared new appetizers and sampled from our new entree list.

What wound up happening was an old-fashioned Sunday family dinner. We shared stories of our lives, our work, our joys and our struggles. We got to know each other on a more real level. And all because we shared some food and brought people together, all via Twitter.

What started as a purpose-driven business tweet-up, done to expose the restaurant's new menu to some Twitter friends and friends of their friends, ended up as a fabulous Sunday family dinner.

Did we achieve our goals? Absolutely. But we got more, A LOT more!

We have real friends who will give us their honest opinion about things, whether we ask for it or not. Twitter users would tweet when they were going to go to dinner at our place, and often even when they were at our restaurant enjoying a meal. Good or bad, this has raised the bar for our restaurant. Guests know if the meal isn't great, and they tweet about it, they can expect us to make it better. And that's exactly what we do. Our guests gave us permission to engage them at their point of experience, and helped us to fine-tune our restaurant items - LIVE!

Notes:

#TwitterWorks – Invite your customers in for a Sunday family dinner. Let them taste all the great stuff you have, and share their honest feedback. Take their feedback and use it to improve your business. Let them take pictures, share stories. Make them feel at home in your space, and they'll make it their own, invite their friends, and become your friends.

#TwitterWorks

Notes:

#TwitterWorks – Be authentic, not automated. Connect with people in a real way.

#TwitterWorks

Create a loyal community of fans.

Special pizzas and burgers created by (and about) our Twitter followers.

While we certainly didn't plan AJ Bombers this way, it has very much become a restaurant that's concept has been built around the suggestions, feedback and total involvement of our guests.

They've shaped the look and feel of the restaurant with their @signs all over every wall and booth, we call it twitffiti. (Get it? Like graffiti, but by tweeters). They really make their mark on the "Cow of Fame" where your name is displayed when you complete one of our Quad burgers. Both of these style of markings inside the restaurant lead guests to show their mark to their friends when they come back. Several guests have "their" booth or "their" seat at the bar. Many of them take photos of their "mark" and use them within their own tweets from the restaurant.

Most importantly, however, our guests have shaped our menu. From Pepper Jack cheese being renamed Pepper Jim cheese in honor of our Foursquare mayor Jim Simon, to our most famous burger, The Barrie Burger - created from an idea from one of our most regular guests, Kate Barrie. Also, it may very well be the ONLY burger with a social media following (see @barrieburger).

The Aj Bombers "Cow of Fame." Eat a Quad burger and you to can write your name on it.

The Barrie Burger. This could be the only burger in the world with its own social media following.

When we opened AJ Bombers, we hoped to feature a burger of the month. It became known as the #BOTM (much easier to tweet). We started out with a plan to do a "seasonal" burger, you know, around the holidays and seasons and such. But Twitter wouldn't allow for such a scripted play, we had guests recommending burger options nearly every day, and some were really great. So we set out to change the #BOTM from Burger of the Month, to it's new meaning: Burger of the Moment. And it works from a sales standpoint as well, because you never know how long one burger's moment may last. Get 'em while they're hot!

The question now is, "How many moments will this burger get?"

A great example is the "Bomber Cristo," our spin on the traditional Monte Cristo sandwich. People asked us, via Twitter, to keep it around a little longer. Of course we're not going to argue with more sales, so we're keeping it around.

Our most popular items go from secret items or #BOTMs to regular menu items within a few weeks of their creation. In the end, it's the extended sense of community of having the ability to create burgers for the restaurant that helps to foster, the real story behind the success of AJ Bombers: It's all about the guests and their interaction with the restaurant. Changing it, shaping it, honestly making it their own.

Twitffiti covers the walls at AJ Bombers.

Streetza Pizza did the same thing with pizzas. What follows are a few fun examples.

THE @TODDZ TWITTER SPAM SLICE
Read before you click. We signed up for some dumb auto-friend thing on Twitter. @toddz was the first to make us aware doing so was a mistake, and that it had resulted in our followers getting a bunch of spam tweets. Once it came to our attention (thank you, @toddz), we changed our password 5 times, and one hour later, everything was back to normal. Thank goodness.

We felt the experience warranted the creation of pizza slice to thank our Twitter followers for their patience. The @toddz pizza slice is loaded with spam (of course!), tomato sauce, pineapple chunks, green peppers, red onions, mozzarella cheese and a special blend of five other cheeses from @WisCheese. We bring this slice to all tweet-ups now.

THE TWEETUPGIRLS HEART BREAKER SLICE
This slice was the brainchild of our Twitter friends, the @tweetupgirls. It's loaded with artichoke hearts, chicken, sun-dried tomatoes, basil, mozzarella cheese and a special blend of five other cheeses from @WisCheese.

THE BREW CREW SAUSAGE RACE SLICE
Our Twitter friend, @jordonm, gets the credit for this home team slice that features all the Klement's racing sausages (a local spectacle of a race that can be witnessed at all home Brewer baseball games). We take the Brat, Hot Dog, Polish, Italian and Chorizo sausages and pile them on our pizza.

THE BREWER'S HILL SLICE
We also decided to do something more local, to be a real "slice" of the neighborhood, using ingredients from the neighborhood. For example, The Brewer's Hill slice. Features the finest locally produced bratwurst, simmered in Blatz beer (orginally brewed in the Brewer's Hill neighborhood), it's loaded with tomato sauce, mozzarella, provolone and parmesan. Served with a side of sauerkraut.

When Streetza goes to a neighborhood, we mention the pizzas on Twitter, raising the profile of his pizza…and the neighborhood!

In addition to mentioning the pizza, which in itself would be pretty usual, Scott also shares links to other cool things in the area, so folks who stop in can have a great next place to go after they finish their pizza. Sometimes it's a link to historical stuff in the neighborhood, and sometimes it's pictures he's taken, between selling slices of pizza, that he gives to the neighborhood association to help them grow stronger.

In essence, Scott became a spokesperson for the neighborhood by sharing links to interesting happenings in the area. And by promoting other businesses in the neighborhood, folks don't see Streetza Pizza as competition and instead welcome the truck with open arms.

Not only does Streetza park in neighborhoods, we create pizzas based on them, and then educate people about the neighborhoods and promote other businesses and events going on in the neighborhoods. Above, Streetza in Humboldt Park in Bay View and in Brewers Hill.

Build Other Characters: Create real life experiences that are remarkable

As our restaurant (AJ Bombers) developed, we found that we often took on different roles when we interacted with our guests on Twitter. This led us to create few different personalities to take on those roles. These are the personalities that we still actively tweet with today:

The Burger Whisperer @burgerwhisperer – We created this Twitter personality to solicit feedback from our guests on the burgers and food they'd like to see us try, and to give them a direct line to the person in charge of actually preparing their meals. It's been a huge amount of fun, and far more successful a social media tool than we could have ever anticipated. Check out the site: theburgerwhisperer.com

THE BURGER WHISPERER

YOU THINK IT UP, WE'LL WHIP IT UP.
AJBOMBERS - MILWAUKEE, WI.

Thee Milwaukee Burger
Here it is, our entry into the Food Wars competition. And while we can't tell you the winner, you can now stop by and taste one for yourself. Topped with Wisconsin Colby/Jack cheese, Nueske's Applewood smoked bacon, and Schlitz onions, yum!

Keeping the winner under wraps helps to give us a shot at the **premier** episode - Season 2 of Food Wars on The Travel Channel, so thanks for understanding.
3 DAYS AGO
3 COMMENTS AND 0 REACTIONS

The real star of Food Wars!
The Barrie Burger was the star of the show today. We're so proud.
3 DAYS AGO
0 COMMENTS AND 0 REACTIONS

Yay, it's Cinco de Mayo
Pepper Jim cheese, with fresh Pico de Gallo - yum!
1 WEEK AGO
1 COMMENT AND 0 REACTIONS

Testing, testing, 1.2.4?
It doesn't always work out the way I hope that it will. The super-fabulous caramelization of the burger just overwhelms the subtlety of the apples and the delicate cheese. Wait, did I just write that! Wayyy too much Food Network for me this week....Oops.
2 WEEKS AGO

"The rivalry between Sobelmans and AJ Bombers is best described as an old school, established "best burger" in Milwaukee joint, running up against the new school, or new kid on the block, very fast to be declared Milwaukee's best 'new' burger joint. I'm telling you, it's a city divided! And both joints have super vocal and fiercely loyal fans to one side or the other. The AJ Bombers supporters are a social media savvy bunch, while the Sobelmans fans are a grass roots angry mob, fuming that someone would threaten the title of their precious hangout."

So here's the scoop: the crew from The Travel Channel show, Food Wars will be in Milwaukee from May 6th through May 8th. Filming one day at each

Fun with Pretzel Buns!
Every once in a while it's fun to combine a few menu items. This one turned out FABULOUSLY! The pretzel flavor is a little strong as a sandwich, but man, does Miller Bakery know how to make a pretzel.....so good.
1 WEEK AGO
1 COMMENT AND 0 REACTIONS

www.theburgerwhisper.com

The Bomb Squad (Drill Sergeant) @bombersquad – We developed this personality long before we actually had an active Twitter account for AJ Bombers. We used the Bomb Squad to introduce our surrounding neighbors to our burgers. We'd bring along a free sample of our sweet potato chips, P-nuts and some T-shirts and and just drop in on their office.

The Bomb Squad and their custom delivery bicycle.

Once we introduced ourselves to these folks, we'd follow up with a scheduled free lunch visit for their office, as well as drop off menus and our burger punch cards in hopes of a) proving the quality of our product, b) fostering new business from our physical neighbors, c) introducing them to our Twitter account.

Souperman @soupermanrules – The concept of The Bomb Squad worked so well for AJ Bombers that we decided it would be fun to give it a shot with our other restaurants, Swig and Water Buffalo, which are in a different Milwaukee neighborhood known as The Historic 3rd Ward. This time, we used our famous and best-in-the world chicken tortilla soup to get our foot in our neighbor's door. This time around, we also additionally employed many social media tactics to further the reach of this promotion. We started by creating the @soupermanrules Twitter personality and RT'ing his tweets to our existing followers to build him a small audience. Then we'd tweet out a call for Souperman, asking who needed to be saved by soup.

Soupermanrules pays a visit to Neroli Salon and Spa's corporate office.

Then, we snapped photos for twitpics, streamed live with Ustream and drew attention to those streams via tweets. We also created lunch punch cards for our visits. Nearly all of these interactions were tweeted simultaneously.

Please allow me to make special mention of the man that did all the heavy lifting in this case, Ryan Packard. Ryan is a very gifted man, blessed not only with the gift of gab, but a personality that shines so brightly that it's nearly impossible to look away. His generosity and personal touch plays an integral role in the continued success of our hospitality company. Thank you Ryan for all that you do.

Mrs AJBombers @mrsajbombers – What started out simply as a way to introduce Angie (Joe's wife) to Twitter turned into a social media experiment in its own right. Angie has developed a following for her Twitter account in the most authentic way possible – she's herself every single tweet along the way. She simply doesn't hold back, whether she's tweeting about being a vegetarian (ironic for the owner of a burger joint), her love of animals, sharing some fun photos or just being the woman I married. No one can tell her story better than the woman behind the tweets herself, so, take it away Angie:

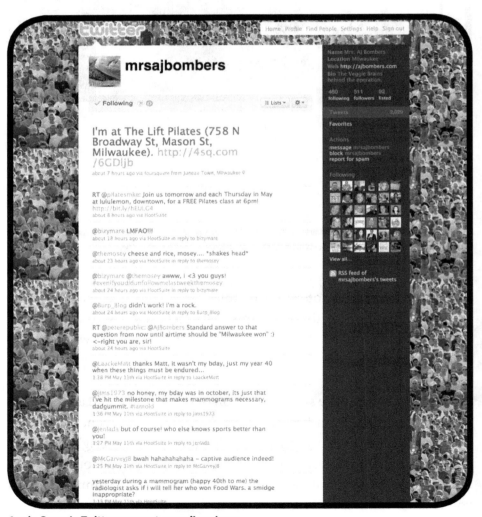

Angie Sorge's Twitter account, mrsajbombers.

I learned to use Twitter when Joe made a "mrsajbombers" account because he saw other wives being represented. I felt like I should be the one speaking, since it was, after all, supposed to be me. I began tweeting with folks on a more personal level about whatever it was they had going on. Sometimes I would get into a discussion with one person, and then more and more people would start chiming in. We'd end up with 8-10 people discussing a topic. It was amazing to be able to pull people with similar thoughts into a conversation without disturbing or alienating those who weren't interested. I've just crossed 500 followers, just from running my mouth!

We planned a tweet-up over the holidays, and it was the first time I was going to be in the same room with many of the people I had had conversations with. Joe asked if I was nervous. I said, "No, it's like walking into a big group of friends that I've never actually seen before."

From left to right: Joe Sorge (AJBombers), Angie Sorge (MrsAJBombers), Scott Baitinger (StreetzaPizza), and Joe Woelfle (BlatzLiquor) at the Tweet-up Holiday Party.

Two people who have been most helpful to Streetza Pizza, Olga Thomas (OlgaThomas) and Harry Castaldo (TKDFool). Their tweets add a lot of charisma and charm to our account.

#TwitterWorks – Get the whole family involved. Let them share their story, and connect with your patrons. It humanizes your restaurant and allows others to get a behind-the-scenes look at what your restaurant does and who is behind your restaurant.

#TwitterWorks

Service recovery - When things don't go as they should.

Sometimes, things don't go as well as we'd like them to. Whether it's an extremely busy day or your staff just isn't on their toes, for whatever reason, sometimes it just doesn't all come together.

Your customers WILL inevitably notice this, and they will inevitably take that experience to their, "megaphone" i.e., their group of friends and followers. Hopefully, they'll clue you in to the fact that they are talking about you, but this is also where your listening skills come into play.

So how do you handle a service gaffe or a guest who's unhappy with their dish? Once again, nearly exactly the same way that you would if you were right there at that guest's table. These great practices of the hospitality industry never get old:

1. Get out in front of the problem, apologize, make NO excuses and admit you made a mistake. (It is NOT your guest's fault.)

2. Offer to "make it right" for your guest, whatever that means for your restaurant.

That's about it – just DO NOT IGNORE the comment. Many life-time customers have been earned entirely due to your ability to resolve their complaint or issue above and beyond their expectations. Wouldn't you rather the story they tell their friends is that yes, they had an issue at this particular restaurant, but you wouldn't believe how great they were in resolving the matter?

I could never have predicted that we'd lose our flattop grill on a Friday morning. (Well, that's not quite true, of course I could have. Doesn't your equipment always seem to need repair on the weekend or after hours? Sheesh. Well, when our main piece of equipment went down on a Friday morning, we had a serious choice to make. We could do what most restaurants would've done, that's either slap up a handwritten sign that said, "Sorry, closed for lunch today" or even try to limp through our lunch service by only serving those items on our menu that we could cook that day, like 25% of the menu.

Instead, I took the issue to our friends on Twitter.

We called the fiasco "operation grill rescue," and took photos of our grill in pieces in the kitchen and attached them to our tweets. I wasn't convinced that would be enough though, as not every customer of ours is a Twitter user, so we went a couple of steps further.

We decided that because it was Friday, we'd invite anyone who walked in the door to start their happy hour early with free beer and peanuts, as much as they'd like, but if they couldn't stay or had to return to work, or that whole drinking-at-lunch thing was frowned upon, we handed them an AJ Bombers branded bag of peanuts to take with them and throw all over their office floor. This was purely guest service. Until I decided to tweet these same intentions.

Almost immediately after I tweeted the details of #operationgrillrescue, a local brewery and friend, Horny Goat Brewery, stepped forward to donate free beer for the cause. I was impressed! How great of them to offer, and they knew I'd be tweeting about their gesture all day as well. I wasn't sure whether that had anything to do with their decision or not.

My last step here was a big one for us that day, both in the social media and business sense. I took my hosting post at the door for lunch, and on this day was ready to explain our situation, but I chose to add the element of a live video event via a great service called Ustream.tv, and even added live chat to the mix.

Most potential guests that day were understanding enough, some were just flat out upset with me as if I'd done it on purpose! While some others happily accepted the free Horny Goat beer and peanuts. The entire exchange was captured live on Ustream. At one point we had nearly 30 viewers, many from offices with multiple people watching me do my best to make lemons out of lemonade. The event spread through Twitter quite quickly. I was getting shout outs of "good luck Joe," "go get em," and "I want my virtual free beer" from not only across the country, but even from our burger friends in London and as far as away as Australia.

In the end, we did get the grill back up and running by late lunch. And while we did disappoint a few guests that day by having to say no (which I HATE to do), more than 20 of the nearly 40 guests that couldn't stay for free beer and peanuts made it back for dinner that very same day. And I still, many weeks later, continue to hear from guests who say, "Hey, I was here that day the grill went down. Did you ever get that fixed?" I smile and tell them their next beer is on the house!

@Milweb1 Hey they carry our product so we definitely will help wherever possibile! :)
1:04 PM Apr 9th via Echofon in reply to Milweb1

We're on our way @AJBombers! And we've got plenty of yummy beer :)
12:46 PM Apr 9th via Echofon

RT @AJBombers: Maybe the grill should go down every day! friends @HornyGoatBrewCo are supplying the FREE BEER for lunch today
11:39 AM Apr 9th via HootSuite

They carry us! #GetwellsoonGrill RT @AJBombers: Let's do this! Free Beer & Free PNut Lunch today Cuz thats all we got #operationgrillrescue
11:16 AM Apr 9th via HootSuite

When the grill went down at AJ Bombers, Horney Goat Brewing helped out by supplying free Horny Goat beer to patrons while they were waiting for it to be fixed.

#TwitterWorks – Remember you're doing all this in front of an audience, so customers can learn your restaurant is great about fixing problems WITHOUT them personally having to experience the error. Take time to seek out these bad experiences and admit you have screwed up...in public.

#TwitterWorks

Cat food isn't mouse flavored.

"If cat food were being sold to cats, it'd be mouse flavored" – Seth Godin
So many products aren't marketed to the end user. Take, for example, all the things Joe does to make kids welcome at AJ Bombers. There are high chairs in plain view. Many customers don't notice them, but customers who have kids see them at lunch…and they come back on the weekend and bring their kids with them.

Joe makes an effort to make kids happy, because happy kids sell parents on the value of coming back to AJ Bombers, over and over again. Joe purposely created a kid-friendly environment from offering the p-nut bombers, to the collection of Big Boys, to the fact anyone can write on the furniture, to….

Notes:

#TwitterWorks – You can learn who your REAL customers are by using Twitter. Cater to them by catering to their kids, and you'll be selling more cat (and restaurant) food than ever before.

#TwitterWorks

It's not just your restaurant anymore, it's everyone's.

We hope that you noticed all those @ signs just inside the cover of this book. We've included their stories, which we hope you can tell, are also OUR stories. And that's the whole point. Social media tools like Twitter allow you to further extend your businesses community, online and in real life at your business. Engage your guests and you will be handsomely rewarded with a business that you can be proud to say your community built!

No one can get to this point – the point any of us are at – without the help of community. Not sure if you've noticed (you will), but Twitter and social media, in general, are overwhelmingly generous and supportive mediums for personal and professional growth. Ask for help! It's out there, and most of our audience wants nothing more than to share, and give real feedback.

Notes:

#TwitterWorks – Invite your customers in for a Sunday family dinner. Let them taste all the great stuff you have, and share their honest feedback. Take their feedback and use it to improve your business. Let them take pictures, share stories. Make them feel at home in your space, and they'll make it their own, invite their friends, and become your friends.

#TwitterWorks

@SKSDesigns @supermanrules @NViousPhotog
@AndrewWech
@buellesbach @sweetfreed @RobertJames1 @pizzakari
@mjburian
@ranpaikard @EllenWinters @loivy @faintstarlit
@impeccableimage
@_TKDFool @stunamisays @booty @Sue Spaight @bulla
@CaitlinMorrall @LauraGraner @karencooksit @SARANDIPITY @DarenMaurer
@Sarabeef @peterepublic @melody-jones
@JOYMAN720 @templon @tweetupgirls
@compujeramey @JMAL18 @mchang01
@SportsBubbler @Bobosnakes @Charno
+ @KateBarrie
@MILWEB1 TheMutes
@accidentalwi @identifyyourself @ashldon88
@ryanschade @joshjs @misterteenwolf @NicholasRies
@danlaske @vitanga @CHRISFROMRACINE
@raffel @edcetera @AndyFrahm @kikibird
@ColinBeal TODDBrink @MeritFrahm @laskeMatt @taraperson @Spanky
@hautwife @beaaahh @LynnCaliachio @andythompson
@milwaukeewave formerly known as @banana
@italianmama

The real reason that #TwitterWorks

Thank you.

is because of you.

@tweetlessA

@Jimo1973

@Spoon

@BrewCityTallB

@KrittaBug

@onmilwaukee

@JungOON

@MarkFairbanks

@EarthAwards

@IRONCUPCAKEMKE

@MattRyan32

@translatorXD

@erica conway

@candid carrie

@milwaukee foodie

@flipeleven

@bombersquad

@deziner

@triveraguy

@triveragirl

@triverabuy

@KStohl

@tourspott

@BlatzLiquor

@AugustinSantiago

@burgerwhisperer

@Yoon Joho

@amyKant

@steveduncan

@SaraSantiago

@Sddbj

@identify-urself

@HappyAlayna

@The Cheap Shots

@Mserita

@Saidoh

@Jonkurozawa

@MRC58

@Brennan MKE

@Kbctourcompany

@haydenakzandee

@the Beer Runner

@Marquette U

115

@agustinsantiago – Augie has a fantastic sense of humor and we love seeing him at AJ Bombers. Unfortunately, on the day of our tweep signing, Augie was rushed to the hospital for an emergency checkup. We were all horribly disappointed at this fact, but he responded in very typical Augie fashion.

@sarasantiago – Sara may be our biggest cheerleader! She's always been there to lend and ear and to try out a new burger. Thanks Sara.

@ShermanJeff – Jeff was one of the first real live Milwaukeeans we met when we moved to Milwaukee in 2000. Not only Milwaukee's biggest evangelist, but a respected leading business owner @OnMilwaukee and voice of a community.

@solessence – Hilary is always willing to lend a hand in helping us to reach more Milwaukee peeps, thanks for that.

@meatpants – Besides having one of the greatest @signs in the Twitter-verse, Ryan has served as a taste tester for many a new item at both AJ-Bombers and Streetza. How do you stay so fit?

@mchang01 – Michael loves to promote others, his generous spirit has led us to look to him first for what's happening with our own businesses out there on "the internets."

@KateBarrie – Here she is, perhaps our most famous Tweep and the brains behind the idea of The Barrie Burger. Kate, we're so happy to call you our friend and customer. Thanks for a great Year One.

@ashdon88 – Ashley is a member of the Original Bomb Squad! One of our opening team and the creator of The Bloody Bomber – Milwaukee's Best Bloody Mary! Ok, 3rd best, but still...

@misterteenwolf – This crazy guy and his significant other @moosesjackson are two of our favorite and most fun customers! Who else grabs an AJ Bombers shirt on his way to the airport, just so he can sport it in Amsterdam.

@chrisfromracine – Chris enjoys AJ Bombers most with her son, "the boy" ..... He loves the Pnut Bombs.

@LaackeMatt – Matt works just up the street at Laacke and Joys, he's basically our neighbor, but not in a Mr. Rogers sort of way. He even has his own burger style, take it to the Matt!

@bananza – Anne has a cult following in Milwaukee on Twitter, a real friend and influencer of many.

@italianmama2 – Is it @lynncaliccho or @italianmama2 today? Lynn has attended each and every event we've ever hosted. Lynn, thanks so much for all your efforts.

@beccaahlf – Another one of our original staff members @AJBombers. Becca works hard and is a budding artist at The Milwaukee Institute of Art and Design. You go Bec.

@milwaukeewave – we love the wave and all the fun promotions between the two of us. Best one to start with: Wave Wednesdays, try The Wave Burger and earn a "buy one get one" ticket voucher for any game.

@ColinDeval – A huge soccer fan in his own right and a participant in our #wbtastetweet. It's been great to get to know you this year Colin.

@ToddBrink – I've always been fascinated with the sheer volume of Todd's followers, then I realized it's all about his blip.fm <http://blip.fm> DJ skills. Thanks for all you do Todd. We love to host the Brink Gang.

@edcetera – if ever there was one person that The Burger Whisperer strives to please, it's Ed. Do not fear the Bit Burger! Also, the inventor of the Edrito and an iPhone app wizard. Ed also enjoys barefoot walks in fresh cut grass and a tall glass of lemonade. Ladies, I think he's single!

@ryanschade – 80s Hair Bands are the tie that binds Ryan and Joe. Not strange to see daily tweets between the two when they hear their favorite 80's tunes. Thanks for playing along Ryan. Great to have your support.

@Milweb1 – Who could imagine that there'd be a social media sign guy? Well here he is! Thanks Nick for all you do for us. Great job!

@SportsBubbler – his most famous tweets with us are, "you may have heard this one before, I'm headed to AJ Bombers for lunch". Love that tweet!

@KatieFelten – Our sister in Social Media. You cannot talk Social Media in Milwaukee without mentioning Katie Felten or MKELive.

@andyfrahm and @merifrahm some of our best buds from the #Bombers Bender Fridays of the Summer of 2009. You guys are so great for putting up with us for so long.

@joshjs – Josh. Likes. Food. Josh. Likes. Beer.

@indentifyyourself + @identify_urself = #tweetupgirls. The hostesses with the mostesess, if you want to organize a tweetup, look no further. Thank you Michelle and Jeanette for all you've done for the advancement of social media in Milwaukee.

@angrae17 + @mserita – you do not see one without the other and we'd have it no other way. A couple of the sweetest girls you could know and always supportive and willing to try new promotions with us.

@MRC58 and @kbctourcompany are some of the most outgoing tweeps around, we're so happy to have their very vocal support. Thank you guys.

@BrennanMKE – Brennan is the most fun, outgoing tech geek we've ever met. And a bit of a foodie! Nice. He's also building the soon to be launched AJ Bombers and Streetza Pizza iPhone apps.

@jonkurozawa – the king of Foursquare in Milwaukee, I have no idea how he keeps a job and is such a great family man at the same time. Maybe that's the key.

@amykant – Talk about energy to spare! Wow, Amy's like the Tasmanian Devil of creativity. You go girl.

@BlatzLiquor – Ahhh, our partner in many crimes, Joe could have assembled his own book on his use of social media in Milwaukee. He is one of the trailblazers and we're proud to call him our partner in many adventures. Joe, do you tweet in the shower?

@SKSDesigns – Shannon has been one of our most vocal supporters on twitter, it's hard to thank you enough for all you share with your world about our businesses. We owe you, big time.

@TKDFool – Our first new restaurant GM that's officially been hired using twitter.

@LauraGainor – Laura has her very own social media success story with @cometbranding using the tool to score herself a gig with the agency while moving to Milwaukee from Charlotte.

@Sawaboof – Our Sarah with an H! So great to have you as our customer, who else could deliver their feedback in such a sarcastic way and actually have it mean something important? Your unique view of the world via Twitter is always refreshing.

@TheMosey – The Twitterverse in Milwaukee would NOT be the same without @TheMosey in it. You'd never know that this razor-bladed tweeter is a family man at heart and one smart dude.

@Sarandipity – The Queen of The Bloody Brunch, and one of the most creative tweeters on the planet. Although, to be honest, I have conferred with a twanslator more than once to decipher your tweets! #youvebeenserved!

@peterpublic – your snarky tweet style and Foursquare activity make for an interesting follow on twitter. The best part is your ability to just tell it like it is. Thanks for that.

@templon – Matt is one of our original influencers, an early adopter so to speak, he interacted with all of us in the Summer of 2009 and introduced us all to the love of his life, Google!

@bullmeister @faintstarlite @judecrawford – Look, it's the Crawford gang! It's always a brighter day when the Crawfords grace our businesses with their presence, we're so happy to have your support.

@pizzakari – The creator of Table Awesome! Thanks for all of your tweets and business over our 1st year.

@msorge – Mike bleeds his own blood! (It must be the last name.) Mike, AJ Bombers is what it is today thanks to your hard work and dedication! It's a JAM Bomb!

@jims1973 – the original Mayor of AJ Bombers on Foursquare and just may be the tweeter that started it all for us. Afterall, his first day tweeting was our first day in business.

@MattRyan32 – from bartender to superstar in minutes! Everyone knows Matt, The Sam to our Cheers.

@TriveraGuy @TriveraGirl – Milwaukee's digital power couple, The Snyders. Always a compliment to have their particpation in our businesses.

@jungbow – our 1st emplyee actually hired via twitter. Her incredible enthusiasm makes any day a fun day!

@ericaconway – Oh boy, Erica, you need your own chapter. No single person has been more involved in all of our businesses.

Phil Gerbyshak

The authors.

PHIL GERBYSHAK
(The Make It Great Guy), Founder, Make IT Great Institute
Phil@twitterworks.tv (@philgerb on Twitter)

5 Words about Phil Gerbyshak
Energetic, helpful, inspiring, enthusiastic, fun

Phil Gerbyshak is the founder of the Make It Great! Institute, and a self-proclaimed relationship geek; someone who knows all the tools, but also knows that people are what really matter in business, and in life.

Phil has been working in the social media space for over five years, and his work on building relationships using blogs was spotlighted in the 2006 book What Nobody Ever Tells You About Blogging and Podcasting: Real Life Advice from 101 People Who Successfully Leverage the Power of the Blogosphere.

Phil is a take-charge kind of guy, not content to passively wait for life to happen to him. Life is what you make of it, and Phil has decided to Make It Great! He has made it his mission in life to help as many people as possible to live the fulfilled, empowered lives they deserve. He has compiled his techniques for living a successful life built on meaningful relationships. He has been elaborating on his Make It Great! philosophy of life at the Make It Great! blog since 2005, and has written over 2000 articles on how to improve your life, your business, and your relationships.

Phil enjoys helping others learn the simple strategies and tactics that make life and organizations great. His latest book #TwitterWorks is focused on understanding and leveraging social media for small businesses and restaurants.

Notes:

#TwitterWorks – Find new customers, fans and friends by building awareness.

#TwitterWorks

Joe Sorge

The authors.

JOE SORGE
Owner - AJ Bombers, Swig, Water Buffalo, Sullivan's, The Smoke Shack
Joe@twitterworks.tv (@ajbombers on Twitter)

Joe was practically born in a restaurant. His family has owned and operated an Italian American restaurant in central New York since June 5, 1951. At the age of 11, he began working there and learned the business from the ground up. Joe then attended Cornell University and earned his BS in Hospitality Management from their world-renowned School of Hotel Administration, with a major in Restaurant Operations and a minor in Entrepreneurship in 1993. His career in the hospitality industry began with a seven-year stint in South Carolina that included working with the House of Blues and two other privately-held hospitality groups. In 2000, Joe and his wife Angie moved to Milwaukee, WI, where they now make their home with their two Bullmastiffs, Ferguson and Isabel. Together, they have built a hospitality company that includes four restaurants (AJ Bombers, Smoke Shack, Swig and Water Buffalo), a bar (Sullivan's) and an event space (The Roasting Room) – all in the downtown area of Milwaukee, WI.

#TwitterWorks – Recently, Joe's work with various social media tools, like Twitter and foursquare, has earned him national recognition by CNN, The Wall Street Journal, The NY Times, Nations Restaurant News, The Travel Channel's – Food Wars, Hospitality 101, Hubspot, TechCrunch, Mashable, Forrester Research, The Business Journal, SoHo Biz Tube, and Twitter Talk Radio, as well as in blogs, case studies and websites around the world.

Notes:

#TwitterWorks – Find new customers, fans and friends by building awareness.

#TwitterWorks

Scott Baitinger

The authors.

SCOTT BAITINGER
Owner - Streetza Pizza, Partner - The Smoke Shack
Scott@twitterworks.tv (@streetzapizza on Twitter)

Scott started working in the restaurant industry when he was 13 years old. By the time he was 17, he had been promoted to the position of head chef. He continued working as a sous chef at Eleanor's on Broad Street in a Milwaukee suburb throughout college. Afterwards, Scott began his career in advertising. Throughout his advertising career, he has won accolades for his creative work, including a BMA Bell best-in-show award for his work with Kohler Company, a Stevie award nomination for work with Markel Insurance and over one hundred other local and national awards for clients, such as GE Healthcare, Cardinal Stritch University, William Grant & Sons and others. He is currently the Creative Director at Mader Communications in Mequon, WI. He also has been teaching advertising and design at the Milwaukee Institute of Art & Design (MIAD) for the past 12 years.

In 2009, he united his passion for great food with his passion for savvy marketing and launched Streetza Pizza. The Milwaukee-based pizza truck has been written about in over 600 articles, referencing their innovative menu, concept and use of social media tools. GQ Magazine named Streetza Pizza one of the 10 best food trucks in the U.S. Time Magazine featured Streetza's perfect pie in the March 28, 2010 issue, and Hospitality 101 called it a "concept we love."

Scott has spoken about the truck, and how all of its success can be attributed to social media, at the American Marketing Association, Milwaukee Interactive Marketing Association and SOHO seminars. He will be presenting at the Pizza Executive Summit and at the National Restaurant Association Show. Streetza is currently in negotiations with a private-equity company interested in launching an additional fleet of 100 trucks throughout the Midwest. Scott owes much of his success to his soon-to-be fiancé Olga Thomas' patience with his schedule while building Streetza.

Notes:

#TwitterWorks – Find new customers, fans and friends by building awareness.

#TwitterWorks

Want more help?

Looking for a little more information about leveraging social media for your business? Visit our book website at http://www.twitterworks.tv

Need a great speaker for an upcoming event? Want a fun interview with one of (or all of) the authors for your blog, magazine, newsletter or TV show? Contact us today to inquire about working with us to build your business, because as you know after reading this book, #Twitterworks, Twitter works.